ideals®
COUNTRY
2006

Dedicated to a celebration of the American ideals of faith in God, loyalty to country, and love of family.

Features

Departments

Cover: The light of sunrise touches the peaks of Mount McGown above a meadow of Rydberg's penstemon in Sawtooth National Recreation Area, Idaho. Photograph by Mary Liz Austin/Donnelly Austin Photography.

Inside front cover: Butterflies do a summer dance in a meadow in this painting entitled THE BUTTERFLIES' HAUNT by William Scott-Myles (1830–1911). Image from Fine Art Photographic Library, Ltd., London/Anthony Mitchell paintings, Nottingham.

IDEALS—Vol. 63, No. 3, May 2006 IDEALS (ISSN 0019-137X, USPS 256-240) is published six times a year: January, March, May, July, September, and November by Ideals Publications, 39 Seminary Hill Road, Carmel, NY 10512. Copyright © 2006 by Ideals Publications. All rights reserved. The cover and entire contents of IDEALS are fully protected by copyright and must not be reproduced in any manner whatsoever. Title IDEALS registered U.S. Patent Office. Printed and bound in the USA. Printed on Weyerhaeuser Husky. The paper used in this publication meets the minimum requirements of American National Standard for Information Sciences—Permanence of Paper for Printed Library Materials, ANSI Z39.48-1984. Periodicals postage paid at Carmel, New York, and additional mailing offices. Canadian mailed under Publications Mail Agreement Number 40010140. POSTMASTER: Send address changes to IDEALS, 39 Seminary Hill Road, Carmel, NY 10512. CANADA POST: Send address changes to Guideposts PO Box 1051, Fort Erie ON L2A 6C7. For subscription or customer service questions, contact Ideals Publications, 39 Seminary Hill Road, Carmel, NY 10512. Fax 845-228-2115. Reader Preference Service: We occasionally make our mailing lists available to other companies whose products or services might interest you. If you prefer not to be included, please write to Ideals Customer Service.

ISBN 0-8249-1308-6   GST 893989236

Visit our website at
www.idealspublications.com

Treasures
Berta Hart Nance

Let those who will possess the gems of earth
And griffin-like their garish treasures guard;
In the icy diamond, the polished shard
Men call the pearl, and in the swollen girth
Of rubies, let them joy and hold of priceless worth
The emerald and turquoise, and the hard
Gilt-gold of topaz, and the silver-barred
Mosaic of opals, lit with fiery mirth.

Be mine, the gold of sunset isles afar,
The rubies of the dawn, with red rays burning,
The pearl and crystal of the winter moon;
Be mine, the silver of the wandering star,
The opal of the tide at moonrise turning,
The emerald of young leaves in breathless June.

June
Helen Jackson

O month whose promise and fulfilment blend
And burst in one! It seems the earth can store
In all her roomy house no treasure more;
Of all her wealth no farthing have to spend
On fruit, when once this stintless flowering end.

A field of zinnias dances with the summer afternoon breeze.
Photograph by Steve Terrill.

Luxuriant Summer

Author Unknown

Luxuriant summer spreads its colored cloak
And covers all the land;
Bright bluebells, sunk in woods of russet oak,
Their blooms expand.

The movements of the bright red-breasted wren,
A lovely melody
Above my house, the thrush and cuckoo's strain
A chorus wakes for me.

The little music-makers of the world,
Chafers and bees,
Drone answer to the tumbling torrent's roar
Beneath the trees.

From gable-ends, from every branch and stem,
Sounds sweetest music now;
Unseen, in restless flight, the lively wren
Flits beneath the hazel bough.

Deep in the firmament the seagulls fly,
One widely-circling wreath;
The cheerful cuckoo's call, the poult's reply,
Sound o'er the distant heath.

The lowing of the calves in summertime,
Best season of the year!
Across the fertile plain, pleasant the sound,
Their call I hear.

Voice of the wind against the branchy wood
Upon the deep blue sky;
Most musical the ceaseless waterfall,
The swan's shrill cry.

No hired chorus, trained to praise its chief,
Comes welling up for me;
The music made for Christ the Ever-young
Sounds forth without a fee.

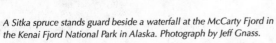
A Sitka spruce stands guard beside a waterfall at the McCarty Fjord in the Kenai Fjord National Park in Alaska. Photograph by Jeff Gnass.

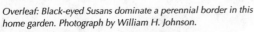
Overleaf: Black-eyed Susans dominate a perennial border in this home garden. Photograph by William H. Johnson.

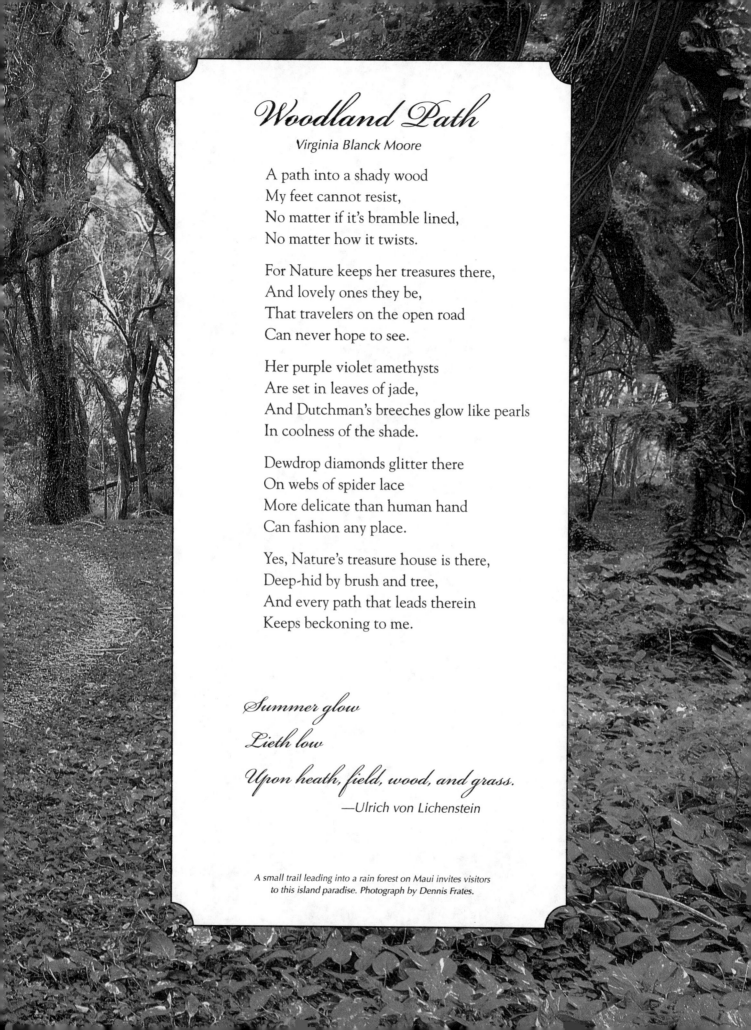

Woodland Path

Virginia Blanck Moore

A path into a shady wood
My feet cannot resist,
No matter if it's bramble lined,
No matter how it twists.

For Nature keeps her treasures there,
And lovely ones they be,
That travelers on the open road
Can never hope to see.

Her purple violet amethysts
Are set in leaves of jade,
And Dutchman's breeches glow like pearls
In coolness of the shade.

Dewdrop diamonds glitter there
On webs of spider lace
More delicate than human hand
Can fashion any place.

Yes, Nature's treasure house is there,
Deep-hid by brush and tree,
And every path that leads therein
Keeps beckoning to me.

Summer glow

Lieth low

Upon heath, field, wood, and grass.
—Ulrich von Lichenstein

A small trail leading into a rain forest on Maui invites visitors to this island paradise. Photograph by Dennis Frates.

The Fair Morning

Jones Very

The clear bright morning, with its scented air
And gaily waving flowers, is here again;
Man's heart is lifted with the voice of prayer,
And peace descends, as falls the gentle rain;
The tuneful birds, that all the night have slept,
Take up at dawn the evening's dying lay,
When sleep upon their eyelids gently crept
And stole with stealthy craft their song away.
High overhead, the forest's swaying boughs
Sprinkle with drops the traveler on his way;
He hears far off the tinkling bells of cows
Driven to pasture at the break of day;
With vigorous step he passes swift along,
Making the woods reecho with his song.

American Forests

John Muir

The forests of America, however slighted by man,
must have been a great delight to God; for they were
the best He ever planted. The whole continent was a
garden, and from the beginning it seemed to be
favored above all the other wild parks and gardens of
the globe. . . .

American forests! The glory of the world!
Surveyed thus from the east to the west, from the
north to the south, they are rich beyond thought:
immortal, immeasurable, enough and to spare for
every feeding, sheltering beast and bird, insect and
son of Adam.

Beautiful columbine blossoms are interspersed among aspens in the Gunnison National Forest in Colorado. Photograph by Carr Clifton.

Summer Songs
Ethel Bryant Cobb

Here are the rippling splash of spring
And cawing blackbird on the wing;
Across the fields comes the sweet refrain
Of gentle winds through golden grain.
The sun sinks lower amid the trees
And leaves the world to twilight's breeze.
Then from the quiet of the hill
Is heard the plaintive cry of whippoorwill;
A round and yellow moon rides high
Through silk-white clouds in a star-flecked sky.
Oh, sing your songs of dreams most rare
While summer's songs are in the air.

Little Brown House
LaRue Price Smith

Wait for me, little brown house in the clearing,
Little brown house at the hem of the hill.
I will come back to roam that deep forest
Where midday is comforting, shadowed, and still.
I will take the worn path that leads from the meadow
And joyously follow the trillium trail.
I will stand heart-high in wild honeysuckle
And linger too long for the first nightingale.
I will find great stands of pink mountain laurel
Guarded by hovering old chestnut trees;
Then pause for a showing of pale lady's slippers;
Breathe deeply and long of the white locust breeze.
I will walk on smooth stones over cold mountain water
And drink from the gourd at Water Cress Spring.
I will sit on a bank strewn with green velvet cushions
And listen, enraptured, to hear nature sing.

*Lady's slippers lift their delicate heads among cattails
and ferns. Photograph by William H. Johnson.*

Summer Journey

Mary Ann Putman

Someday when the gray quails
Are voices calling low,
And the day is like a painting
I saw once, long ago,
I shall leave this paved street
To hike through country roads
Where the air is bittersweet
And the hay is tawny loads;
Where clouds through plum branches
Are white and ragged wreaths,

And the only sound of rushing
Is the traffic of the leaves;
Where all the hills are gnome-green,
Chestnut-colored, rust,
And spotted cows are slow trains
Moving through the dust—
Someday when the gray quails
Are voices calling low,
And the day is a pastoral,
Summer soft and slow.

A Summer Walk

Anne Campbell

The narrow lane behind the barn
Led to the mystery of wood
And meadow. Grandmother would warn
Us not to stray too far abroad.
But often we would rive the cows,
My brother walking close to me,
And after we had left them, browse
Through the deep wood joyfully.

The cows, turned out to pasture, fed
Upon the lush green meadowland;
But we who saw the wood ahead
Were drawn by nature's giving hand.
And often dreaming of release
From adult cares that daily block
My path, in memory of peace,
Again I take that summer walk.

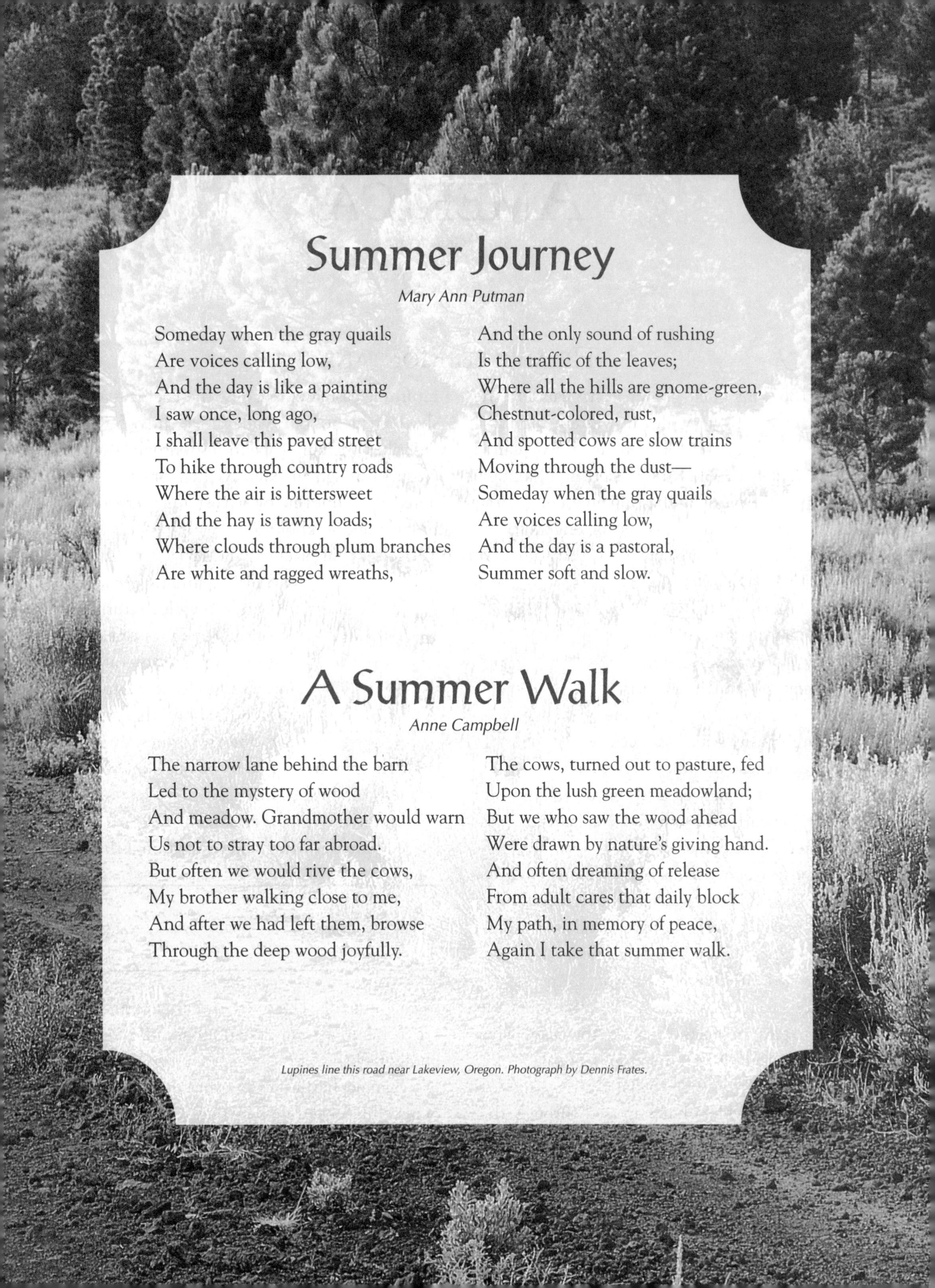

Lupines line this road near Lakeview, Oregon. Photograph by Dennis Frates.

HOMETOWN AMERICA

Susan Graveley

HELMVILLE, MONTANA

In 1867, my great-grandparents came to the Blackfoot River valley in western Montana and helped settle a little town called Helmville. The Gold Rush was on, and Montana was full of new arrivals dreaming of riches.

My great-grandparents were among those who saw something more precious than gold in Helmville. They looked around them—at the vast, fertile prairies and at the Rocky Mountains rising in the distance—and decided that the land was Helmville's true treasure. So my ancestors became ranchers instead of miners. They built homes, raised families, and put down the solid roots that nearly a century and a half later still sustain their descendants.

For five generations my family has lived in Helmville. We have watched the seasons flow by like the mighty Blackfoot River. And as Helmville has remained, so we have remained, our history intertwined with that of the town.

Long before my family arrived, this valley was home to great numbers of Native Americans. They called the trail through the valley Cokahlahishkit, which means "road to the buffalo."

Other travelers have crossed through this valley too. In July of 1806, Meriwether Lewis, his faithful dog, Seaman, and a party of nine men—returning east after reaching the Pacific—made a short visit to our valley. On July 5, Lewis described the landscape in his journal: "the road passing through an extensive high prairie [is] rendered very uneven by a vast number of little hillocks and sinkholes."

After that brief encounter with the history of the expanding American nation, the valley returned to the time-tested routines of its native inhabitants—at least for another half-century. In the 1860s came the prospectors and the mines, and after that, the ranchers. The town of Helmville was officially established in 1872.

Helmville today is a town shaped by its rugged natural setting and the seasonal rhythms

---

For five generations my family has lived in Helmville.

---

of ranching life. The town's rituals and traditions are as familiar to me as an album of old family photographs.

Summer has always meant work. The summers of my childhood were punctuated by daily chores and full of activities. I helped my family with the milking; I rode horses and chased cows. Most of my playmates were cousins. Summer never lasted long enough.

Today, during the long days of July and August, Helmville is alive with the sounds of machinery as ranchers gather hay to feed their cows during the coming winter. The calves, however, are ignorant of winter's looming hardship; they graze contentedly.

Each fall, most of the calves leave Helmville on lumbering trucks headed east. In the quiet after the roar of the trucks fades, we hear the plaintive calls of the mother cows.

Photograph courtesy of Larry Dodge.

In the autumns of my childhood, school was held in a two-room bulding. We students had the responsibilities of a janitor; we did the sweeping and the cleaning ourselves before returning home. For refreshment, we poured water from the pump well into a large crock with a spigot at the bottom.

In winter, our pastureland turns into a stark white landscape broken only by lines of cattle eating hay dropped from ranchers' wagons. On branding and shipping days, students would stay home from school to help. But sunny days meant sledding on the schoolhouse hill.

Now the winters bring the muffled hum of snowmobiles and the familiar, joyful squeals of children coasting down the schoolhouse hill. The school plays during the Christmas season remain the social event of the year. And as always, the friendship of our neighbors helps to carry us through long winters.

In spring, baby calves bring our pastures to life again after the long, snowy winter. They prance about, followed closely by their mothers. The grass is green, the days are long, and the air smells fresh.

On warmer spring days, my friends and I would pick wildflowers on the same hill we used for sledding. And at Easter, the town's children still gather at the local cemetery for an egg hunt.

From this peaceful spot I can look northward to a magnificent view of the Bob Marshall Wilderness. I can look out across the valley floor and see green meadows dotted with golden haystacks. If I am lucky, I might see some of Helmville's abundant wildlife.

Standing in our cemetery, I can imagine Helmville changing through the years, as the sounds of horses whinnying and buggies rattling down dusty trails gave way to the roar of cars and trucks on paved roads. But I can also feel how much life in Helmville is the same. Three generations of our family have come and gone, but at home our family's fifth generation of Helmville ranchers—my children—are at work alongside their father.

In the 1860s, my eight great-grandparents crossed the Atlantic to America and then found their way to Montana. They came by wagon train and, in one case, by foot; but their travels ended once they saw this beautiful valley. Like me, they could not imagine living anywhere else.

My Childhood

Della Taylor Tuttle

Backward, my memory goes even still
To the big beech trees and the house on the hill,
To chestnuts, walnuts, wild grapes on the vine;
To persimmons, pawpaws, and muskadines;
Moss-covered rocks and cool clear springs;
To wildflowers blooming and grapevine swings.

There were brooks to wade and hills to climb,
Caves to explore with no thought of time,
Barefoot and carefree, with heart always merry,
Healthy and happy with never a worry.
What a great joy to play with sisters and brothers,
And God's best gift, my father and mother.

If God would grant me the gift
To turn back my years on this earth
To the carefree days of my childhood
And make me aware of their worth,
It would mean more to me than all riches,
More than all earth's fine gold,
To return to the days of my childhood
And the beautiful times of old.

Nature, like a kind and smiling mother, lends herself to our dreams and cherishes our fancies.
— Victor Hugo

Lupines overflow a field near Mount Adams and Mount Jefferson in the Presidential Range of the White Mountains, New Hampshire. This range is the United States' greatest contiguous alpine area east of the Mississippi. Photograph by William H. Johnson.

A MESSAGE FOR FATHER

Craig E. Sathoff

I am no more the little boy
You bounced upon your knee
And thrilled with songs and olden chants
And tales of mystery.

But, Father, I am guided still,
Much more than words can tell,
By your desire to see tasks through
And do what is done well.

Your caring smile, your love of life,
Your kind and patient ways
Are guideposts which I shall attempt
To honor all my days.

The gifts you gave to your small son
Were not found in a store,
But, Father, now I use them still
Each year, just more and more.

The words that a father speaks to his children in
the privacy of home are not heard by the world,
but, as in whispering galleries, they are clearly
heard at the end, and by posterity.
—Jean Paul Richter

This flower garden in Wisconsin is proudly claimed by "Dad."
Photograph by Darryl E. Beers.

THANK YOU, FATHER

Gail Brook Burket

Thank you for love, which was my firm protection
Against the perils that endangered me.
Thank you for your responsible concern and care,
Providing me with home, food, clothing, and the fun
Of special treats, toys, and exciting outings
That gave a glow to childhood years
And filled my mind with memories,
Which still awaken happiness when I recall them.
Thank you for helping me become aware
That I have individual worth and dignity.
Thank you for opening my eyes to natural wonders
And pointing out that the splendor of the sun and stars,
Fields, mountains, woodlands, and unbounded plains
Is not more worthy of profoundest admiration
Than the incredible perfection of each flake of snow and filament of moss.

Thank you for giving me a deep appreciation
For the beauty found in music, buildings, paintings,
In statues, fabrics, gardens, and designs.
Thank you for introducing me to books,
A treasure-trove of wisdom and delight.
Thank you for fostering a pride in family
That spurred my young resolve to wear my name with grace.
Thank you for encouraging my mind to grow
And letting me develop latent skills.
Thank you for showing me the value of good work,
Demanding that I do my very best in every task,
And expecting me to complete each assignment faithfully.
Thank you for setting a good example
Of civic enterprise and firm integrity.

Thank you for insisting that being myself was not enough—
I must be myself but always at my best.
Thank you for teaching me to worship
And giving me the spiritual perception
That lets me live, abiding in God's goodness.

*Daisies on the table announce summer in this pleasant family
kitchen. Photograph by Jessie Walker.*

My Father

Hilda Butler Farr

If God had let me choose from men
The one I'd like to be my dad,
I would have chosen someone kind
Who made the best of what he had.
I would have asked that he possess
A hand of strength, a pleasant smile,
And be a person children loved,
Who knew best how to meet a trial.

I would have hoped he'd understand
A daughter who is just like me,
And that he'd share my dreams and hopes,
Whatever they would chance to be.
And He whose wisdom never fails
Bestowed on me the best He had—
A man with all these traits and more,
The man I fondly call my dad.

A Tribute

Sherry Kuyt

If I know that God is loving,
That the best of gifts He gives;
If I know about His judgment
And how freely He forgives;
If I know He's always with me,
That He's faithful, wise, and true;
If I know God's like a father,
It's because, Dad, I know you.

Roses provide a beautiful border for this front door in Portsmouth, New Hampshire. Photograph by William H. Johnson.

SOMEONE TO REMEMBER

Anne Kennedy

MY FATHER'S PATIENCE

I recently completed work on a production of *The Sound of Music*, a play wherein the father of seven children is a retired naval officer and runs his household as he would a shipload of unruly recruits. When cast members discovered that my father was also a naval officer, they conjured images of my brothers and me marching down the steps of our various military quarters, sporting matching sailor suits, and shouting our names when prompted by a staccato whistle or angry bark. I laughed it off, but, looking back, I can see how Dad might have been tempted to follow the Captain von Trapp model.

My father grew up in an environment where planning and preparedness were unquestioned. My grandfather, a former navy pilot, encouraged his sons to become Eagle Scouts, and both boys subsequently earned ROTC scholarships, joined their father's fraternity, and became officers in the United States Navy.

My father's life is a remarkable testament to the benefits of planning. I recall cross-country trips when Dad woke everyone before daybreak so we could be "in the stream headed fair" by 6 A.M. and fit in two good hours of driving before breakfast. At home, Dad set all our clocks ahead at intervals. On Sundays he shepherded us out of the house before sunup to make the first service at church. We were early to everything.

Because his job took him out of our lives for long periods, Dad became something of a special-occasion parent who inspired a respectful awe. He must have been uncomfortable with this distance, because, when my brothers were in elementary school and I was only four, Dad announced we would begin a new tradition—he would take each of us out once a month for a one-on-one date wherever we wanted to go. These "special times" grew into the foundation of a deeper relationship with our father.

Despite his penchant for planning and agendas, my father developed an incredible amount of

---

He never filled our times together with probing inquiries or parental advice. He simply listened.

---

patience and enthusiasm for his children's meandering whims. He was equally accepting of "I want to just bum around the mall and look for skateboard wheels," as he was of "Let's see *Honey I Shrunk the Kids* again!" Whatever we did, Dad followed our lead. He never filled our times together with probing inquiries or parental advice. He simply listened. One night a month, he threw away his planner and we knew he was on our side.

As I entered high school, this fatherly patience only increased. Dad drove me to school every day on his way to work. A man quiet by nature, he valued serenity in the morning. But I had drama to work through, teachers to complain about, and boys to consider. I also habitually forgot to take inventory of my schoolbooks until we were on the road, and I more than once meekly asked him to return home so I could retrieve *Romeo and Juliet* or

At home, Dad set all our clocks ahead at intervals.

my calculus text. Pulling a U-turn, he would recite the balcony scene as a kind of Three Stooges routine. When I returned with book in hand, we were ten minutes late, but laughing. He daily reminded me that I was his priority—getting to work on time was only icing on the cake.

Since I have left home, I have noticed my father's patience in new ways. When I announced I would major in creative writing and pursue a career in theater, my dad, the engineer, told me to go for it. And when I performed in my first college production, a dark, two-and-a-half-hour *Macbeth*, he took time off, flew from Honolulu to Seattle, and caught two shows, even though I had no lines and spent most of the show lurking through stage fog, covered in black muslin. Afterwards, he told me I was wonderful, but wondered why we had left out his favorite line: "Wherefore art thou, Romeo?"

A friend once told me she avoids calling her father because he invariably peppers her with advice, then demands to know what she is doing with her life. I remember wondering what makes my father so different. I am certain he worries about me, as most parents do, but he is confident that if I have an issue I will tell him because, as he often reminds me, "I'm in your corner, Sweetheart."

Last week he was in town for a few days, and we arranged to meet at 7:30 for breakfast at a local diner. At 7:35, I awoke with a jolt and frantically called Dad, apologizing and assuring him that I would be there as soon as possible.

"Don't worry, Sweetheart, I can wait. Just be careful on the roads. It's cold out there."

I am who I am. And my father still patiently loves me.

Photograph by Jessie Walker.

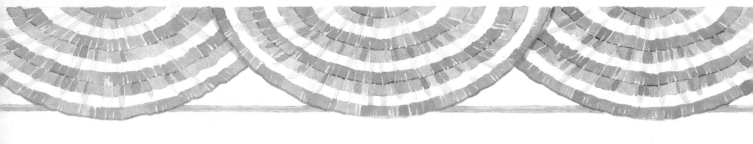

A Tribute to Fathers

Iris W. Bray

Father labors for our needs,
Yet finds the time to spare
To build our hopes and share our dreams,
And still has time for prayer.

We marvel at his courage, which
Dissolves our doubts and fears.
Somehow, he gathers sunbeams
And he swaps them for our tears.

A father's love has patience
And understanding, too,
When we hurt or disappoint him
By the things we say or do.

His arms are always open
With a love that will not fail
And steadfast strength to lean upon
When the trials of life prevail.

For many years his presence
Is a blessing set apart;
Then, through cherished memories,
He lives on within the heart.

Legacy

Helen Darby Berning

Although he was a quiet man
And I a chatterbox,
He seemed to like my skipping pace
When we took our Sunday walks.

The emerald banks along the creek
Where the purplest violets grew,
The daisy field, the walnut grove
Were wonders that my father knew.

A pine-tree cone, a square of moss,
A nest blown from a tree,
Acorn berets, and lucky stones
Were treasures, all for free.

I pressed the fronds of happiness
In the album of the years,
Then added the thorn of sorrow
To the once-shared souvenirs.

Today I gathered violets
And found in the quiet glen
A yesterday, long held in trust,
For a little girl of ten.

Sunshine, straw hats, and a basket of home-baked food—everything needed for a summer picnic is here. Photograph by Dianne Dietrich Leis/Dietrich Leis Stock Photography.

Remembered Joy
Gertrude Dicks

My heart remembers joyful things like strawberries in June,
The hush of evening when the day gives way to summer's moon.
The rain that breaks the driest spell and returns the earth to green
Will bring the same refreshing air when I relive the scene.

Deep in the pockets of my heart these things are hidden well,
But when I bring them into view—what stories they can tell.
They speak of children in the hay where Tabby liked to hide
New members of her family and purr at them in pride.

They spin a bit of mystery and weave the yarn until
There's much to reminisce about that age makes better still.
And yet it seems a joyful heart will always find a way
To add each happy moment to dreams of yesterday.

The Country Path
LaVerne P. Larson

On such a lovely summer day
My feet would walk a country way
Through fields and forests by a stream.
On this path I'd muse and dream
Where I could view the trees and grass
And little animals that pass
With gentle breezes on my cheek.
The country pathway I would seek,
With shafts of sunlight pouring down
To give the earth a golden crown;
I'd hear the birds with sweetest song
And count my blessings all day long.
On such a summer day as this
The country path has heaven's kiss.

*A meadow near the Mazama Ridge in Mount Rainier National
Preserve, Washington, is decorated with alpine flowers.
Photograph by Terry Donnelly/Donnelly Austin Photography.*

A Day in June

James Russell Lowell

And what is so rare as a day in June?
Then, if ever, come perfect days;
Then Heaven tries earth if it be in tune,
And over it softly her warm ear lays:
Whether we look, or whether we listen,
We hear life murmur, or see it glisten;
Every clod feels a stir of might,
An instinct within it that reaches and towers,
And, groping blindly above it for light,
Climbs to a soul in grass and flowers;

The flush of life may well be seen
Thrilling back over hills and valleys;
The cowslip startles in meadows green,
The buttercup catches the sun in its chalice,
And there's never a leaf nor a blade too mean
To be some happy creature's palace;
The little bird sits at his door in the sun,
Atilt like a blossom among the leaves,
And lets his illumined being o'errun
With the deluge of summer it receives;

Now is the high-tide of the year,
And whatever of life hath ebbed away
Comes flooding back with a ripply cheer,
Into every bare inlet and creek and bay;
Now the heart is so full that a drop overfills it,
We are happy now because God wills it;
No matter how barren the past may have been,
'Tis enough for us now that the leaves are green;
We sit in the warm shade and feel right well
How the sap creeps up and the blossoms swell;

We may shut our eyes, but we cannot help knowing
That skies are clear and grass is growing;
The breeze comes whispering in our ear,
That dandelions are blossoming near,
That maize has sprouted, that streams are flowing,
That the river is bluer than the sky,
That the robin is plastering his house hard by;
Joy comes, grief goes, we know not how;
Everything is happy now,
Everything is upward striving;

'Tis as easy now for the heart to be true
As for grass to be green or skies to be blue—
'Tis the natural way of living:
Who knows whither the clouds have fled?
In the unscarred heaven they leave no wake;
And the eyes forget the tears they have shed,
The heart forgets its sorrow and ache;
The soul partakes the season's youth,
And the sulphurous rifts of passion and woe
Lie deep 'neath a silence pure and smooth,
Like burnt-out craters healed with snow.

Purple coneflowers dot the meadow near Mount Adams at Trout Lake in Washington. Photograph by Terry Donnelly/Donnelly Austin Photography.

Simple Things
Ernest Jack Sharpe

These things of life I love to see:
Sunlight filtered through a tree,
A swallow flying in the sky,
Wind-swept waves of growing rye.

These things of life I love to feel:
The tug of trout against my reel,
Rushing water over my feet,
Breezes tempering summer's heat.

These things of life I love to hear:
A singing thrush with notes so clear,
The scrunch of leaves beneath my tread,
Raindrops as I lie in bed.

These things of life I love to smell:
The rich, moist earth of shady dell,
Wood smoke, roses, new-mown hay,
Sweet-scented breeze at close of day.

Simple things, but those I love,
All furnished by the One above.

A Day Upriver
Edith Shaw Butler

Breathe in this quietness of earth and sky,
The river shining in the summer sun
As wavelets lap the shore and willows sigh.
Such hours, such lovely hours are halcyon.
The sky is very blue, this summer day;
The lazy white clouds hardly move at all.
I watch two bright green dragonflies at play;
I hear, far off, a crow's discordant call.
The river bank is edged with pickerelweed,
Blue vervain, and the pearly arrowhead.
A day like this can fill the heart's deep need
For something more than meat and daily bread.
A hidden cricket chirps, a wood thrush sings;
God gives His peace in common, simple things.

Sailboats stand ready for the perfect sailing day at Bayfield, Wisconsin, the gateway to Apostle Islands National Lakeshore on Lake Superior. Photograph by Ken DeQuaine.

BITS & PIECES

Science and art may invent splendid modes of illuminating the apartments of the opulent; but these are all poor and worthless compared with the light which the sun pours freely, impartially, over hill and valley, which kindles daily the eastern and western sky. . . .

—*William Ellery Channing*

The glorious sun
Stays in his course, and plays the alchemist:
Turning, with splendour in his precious eye,
The meagre cloddy earth to glittering gold.

—*William Shakespeare*

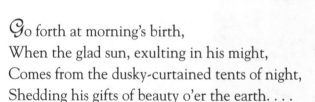

Go forth at morning's birth,
When the glad sun, exulting in his might,
Comes from the dusky-curtained tents of night,
Shedding his gifts of beauty o'er the earth. . . .

—*Emma Catharine Embury*

How beautiful is morning!
How the sunbeams strike the daisies,
And the kingcups fill the meadow
Like a golden-shielded army
Marching to the uplands fair.

—*Dinah Maria Mulock Craik*

*L*ight is the first of painters.
　　　—*Ralph Waldo Emerson*

*F*airest of lights above!
Thou sun, whose beams adorn the spheres,
And with unwearied swiftness move,
To form the circles of our years.
　　　—*Isaac Watts*

*T*he earliest minister of the Almighty, who
chose thee for His shadow; thou chief star,
centre of many stars, thou dost rise, and
shine, and set in glory!
　　　—*George Gordon, Lord Byron*

*A*nd the morning pouring everywhere
Its golden glory on the air . . .
　　　—*Henry Wadsworth Longfellow*

Through My Window

Pamela Kennedy

A Place in the Country

When I was about ten, my parents decided to look for a "place in the country" where they could spend weekends and eventually some vacation time. The first thing you need to understand is that they only had a few thousand dollars to spend; the next thing is that my father and mother were self-employed. They worked together in a small insurance agency, and my dad worked six days a week. Whatever they found had to be within reasonable driving distance and fairly cheap. And then there was the issue of seafood. My mother loves seafood, so she was most interested in finding a place where she could get oysters, clams, crabs, and shrimp—preferably for free! We set out on a rainy February day to search for the place of their dreams.

At ten, my main interest was in the motel where we got to stay overnight. I recall slogging from one piece of property to the next in an unrelenting, cold drizzle, roaming through musty-smelling cabins, and listening to a woman who talked about things I had no interest in, like escrow and titles and tideland rights. But the individually wrapped bars of pink Camay soap and the little bottles of hand lotion back at the Drift Inn Motel were another matter altogether. That was luxury!

At the end of the weekend, my parents purchased, for $2500 in cash, fifty feet of unimproved waterfront property on Hood Canal, a salt-water inlet of Puget Sound, about a two-hour drive from Seattle. They were thrilled. I was unimpressed.

The beach was covered with oysters, sharp and unrelenting, and featured a fifteen-foot-high dirt bank that butted against the highway. At high tide the beach completely disappeared

---

We water-skied, fished, swam, and ate tons of succulent oysters, clams, and Dungeness crabs dredged from the canal's silty bottom.

---

under several feet of salt water. It wasn't quite what I had pictured as a lovely place in the country. I would have been much happier, I suggested, with a permanent unit at the Drift Inn Motel.

Initially, we had to synchronize our visits with the tides. We'd rush to the canal, scoot down the bank with our supplies, and set up a fire pit on the beach. Mom gathered oysters and clams, both of which were undeniably abundant, and we'd steam them open on a grate over the fire. I collected clamshells and made elaborate seaside manors featuring pools and verandas for the tiny rock crabs I caught. Our picnics ended abruptly when the incoming tide began lapping at the coals of our fire. Then we'd pack up our belongings and scramble back up the bank to the car, heading home for another week.

We water-skied, fished, swam, and ate tons of succulent oysters, clams, and Dungeness crabs dredged from the canal's silty bottom. Even I had to agree it was a much better venue than the Drift Inn Motel!

My husband and I and eventually our three children all spent vacation time at the canal. The kids delighted in fishing, swimming, and finding shells to build habitats for little crabs. After some coaxing, they even acquired a taste for the abundant seafood on the shore. My father passed away over a dozen years ago and my mother, concerned about maintenance responsibilities, gave us the property.

The house trailer, about forty years old, had seen better days, but building codes in the area were extremely limiting. It took a creative architect, a fearless builder, diligent environmentalists, and unremitting patience, but we were finally able to construct a cabin on the same site where the trailer had stood for so long. This is the first summer we will be able to stay there, and I look forward to sitting on the deck with my husband, as my mother and dad did for so many years, watching the sunset and awaiting the twinkle of the first evening star.

Over the past five decades, my parents' dreams have become my own; and I hope that if my children marry and have families, they will one day bring them to the canal.

The beach is still covered with oysters and clams, the crab pot still yields its delicious bounty, and I suspect there are tiny crabs hiding under the rocks, just waiting for some little girl or boy to build a terraced manor, complete with a clamshell stairway and a swimming pool, at this lovely little "place in the country."

When I was in junior high, my folks had enough saved to build a bulkhead on the property. This twelve-foot-high wall, backfilled with dirt, gave us a flat area on which to park the car, set up our barbecue, and laugh at the tide as it climbed up the wall, never reaching more than a couple of feet from the top. My dad couldn't wait to find a used house trailer to park on the bulkhead so we could have a "real vacation place." Over the years my parents added a deck that extended over the edge of the concrete bulkhead and, much to my delight, a motorboat!

I spent most of my summer weekends during high school and college with friends at the beach.

Original artwork by Doris Ettlinger.

Midsummer

John Townsend Trowbridge

Oh, softly on you banks of haze,
Her rosy face the Summer lays!

Becalmed along the azure sky,
The argosies of cloudland lie,
Whose shores, with many a shining rift,
Far off their pearl-white peaks uplift.

Through all the long midsummer day
The meadow-sides are sweet with hay.
I seek the coolest sheltered seat,
Just where the field and forest meet—

Where grow the pine trees tall and bland,
The ancient oaks austere and grand,
And fringy roots and pebbles fret
The ripple of the rivulet.

I watch the mowers, as they go
Through the tall grass, a white-sleeved row.
With even stroke their scythes they swing,
In tune their merry whetstones ring.

Behind the nimble youngsters run
And toss the thick swaths in the sun.
The cattle graze, while, warm and still,
Slopes the broad pasture, basks the hill;

And bright, where summer breezes break,
The green wheat crinkles like a lake.

The butterfly and humblebee
Come to the pleasant woods with me;

Quickly before me runs the quail;
Her chickens skulk behind the rail;
High up the lone wood-pigeon sits,
And the woodpecker pecks and flits.

Sweet woodland music sinks and swells,
The brooklet rings its tinkling bells,
The swarming insects drone and hum,
The partridge beats its throbbing drum.

The squirrel leaps among the boughs
And chatters in his leafy house.
The oriole flashes by; and, look!
Into the mirror of the brook,

Where the vain bluebird trims his coat,
Two tiny feathers fall and float.
As silently, as tenderly,
The down of peace descends on me.

Oh, this is peace! I have no need
Of friend to talk, of book to read:
A dear Companion here abides;
Close to my thrilling heart He hides;

The holy silence is His Voice:
I lie and listen, and rejoice.

*Paintbrush and sweet vetch color the landscape at Glacier Bay
National Park and Preserve in Alaska. Photograph by Carr Clifton.*

Golden Day

Ruth B. Field

There was a path through meadows of red clover,
Where the warbler wove his thread of gold.
Above, sheep-clouds on blue gamboled over,
And happiness was here to have and hold.

A golden day, beauty-touched with shadows
Like misty lace upon the meadow green,
And, nearby, in the sun-flecked crystal shallows,
Silver minnows stirred the water's sheen.

Upon a low and emerald-shadowed branch,
A small bird paused with his tenuous hold,
Pouring on the air an avalanche
Of notes that matched the day's own shining gold.

Bright laughter and the softly purling sound
Of water sprites within the dancing stream,
And daisy eyes, wide-staring, on the ground
All interwoven like a rainbow dream.

A summer day, a song upon the air
That magically returns and can instill
The heart with sudden dreams—no matter where
You have roamed, you cannot rest until

Once again the green and sunswept meadows
That you have known so tenderly enfold
Your heart with peace, while the trees' cool shadows
Trace lovely patterns on a day of gold.

*Balsamroot and lupines fill the McCall Point Trail in the Tom McCall
Nature Preserve on Rowena Crest, above the Columbia River in Oregon.
Photograph by Mary Liz Austin/Donnelly Austin Photography.*

The Blackbird

Frederick Tennyson

How sweet the harmonies of afternoon!
The blackbird sings along the sunny breeze
His ancient song of leaves and summer boon;
Rich breath of hayfields streams thro' whispering trees;
And birds of morning trim their bustling wings
And listen fondly—while the blackbird sings.

How soft the lovelight of the west reposes
On this green valley's cheery solitude,
On the trim cottage with its screen of roses,
On the gray belfry with its ivy hood,
And murmuring mill-race, and the wheel that flings
Its bubbling freshness—while the blackbird sings.

The Old Squire

Wilfrid Scawen Blunt

I like the calm of the early fields,
The ducks asleep by the lake,
The quiet hour which nature yields
Before mankind is awake.

I like the pheasants and feeding things
Of the unsuspicious morn;
I like the flap of the wood-pigeon's wings
As she rises from the corn.

I like the blackbird's shriek and his rush
From the turnips as I pass by,
And the partridge hiding her head in a bush,
For her young ones cannot fly.

I like these things, and I like to ride,
When all the world is in bed,
To the top of the hill where the sky grows wide
And where the sun grows red.

A farmstead near La Crosse, Wisconsin, rests peacefully in the summer landscape. Photograph by Darryl R. Beers.

COUNTRY CHRONICLE

Lansing Christman

OLD BARNS

Old barns are like old scribes. They write their rhythmic lines out in the fields far back from the road. They stand alone, surrounded by the land they once served. Theirs is a script that has lasted well, a chronology of life and time, a journal of the years, a record of the seasons and of harvests from the fields.

The vintage structures represent generations of men who followed the plow, year after year. They were men of dreams who loved the land. They chose to live close to it.

Old barns have a rustic elegance when the wilderness starts creeping back to the doors. New trees spring up nearby. Grass grows, and the weeds. And they go to seed. Vines inside the structures send out their tendrils, seeking a foothold in the cracks and crevices in their quest for light.

These aging relics continue to endure despite their sagging sills, loose siding, and roofs ripped and torn by the winds. They reveal a rich mellow beauty, the beauty of an artist's dream. They have been burnished by sun and winds and rain, by ice and snow. Now they wear a sheen that glistens in the sun.

I have an affinity with old barns. I played in barns as a boy and worked in them as a man. On rainy summer afternoons, the raindrops on the shingled roof sent me off to sleep, while swallows chattered overhead.

I sense the antiquity of old barns when I place my hands upon their weathered boards. They speak to me. I sense the rhythm of the earth and the flowing music of the hills. I sense their origin long ago in a primitive forest of whispering pines.

The author of four books, Lansing Christman has contributed to IDEALS *for more than thirty years. Mr. Christman has also been published in several American, international, and braille anthologies. He lives in rural South Carolina.*

An old barn is a perfect backdrop for orange tiger lilies.
Photograph by William H. Johnson.

HONEYSUCKLE

Lucille Crumley

Even as the hills endure,
The white fragrance shall ever stay
Within my heart—nor years can lure
Each lovely memory away.
Precious is the summer, dear the time
The white and yellow waxy blooms return
On sweet, honeysuckle vines that climb
My doorway trellis. Long hours burn
With desire for voices that are stilled
And the welcoming doorway trellis
Where honeysuckle blooms are spilled.
Even as the mountains stand,
The honeysuckle will, each year,
Fling its fragrance sweet
From eternity to here.

*What a pity flowers can utter no sound—
a singing rose, a whispering violet, a
murmuring honeysuckle—oh, what a
rare and exquisite miracle would these be!*
—Henry Ward Beecher

This garden in Neskowin, Oregon, is carefully tended.
Photograph by Steve Terrill.

A Summer Day
Frances Heighton

Sun peeking over the hilltop,
Roses caressed by the dew,
A sea of bright morning glories
Of every imaginable hue,
Corn in the field, gently nurtured
By the sun and the soft falling rain,
Meadows all sounding with new songs,
And daisies soon to be made into chains,
New earth just bursting with life, and
The laughter of children at play—
I am happy because these are part of
This beautiful, warm summer day.

Summer Magic
Viney Wilder

I caught a magic summer day—
A butterfly with gossamer wings.
Alas, too soon it flew away,
But, oh, it left me lovely things
To store against November's chill,
To hold against a wintry sky
Where memory may walk at will
And all the somber world defy.

Brown-eyed Susans and poppies provide bright color beside this garden arbor.
Photograph by Darryl R. Beers.

Morning Glory
June Sensenig

When the night's been long and weary
And I've sought for sleep in vain,
All my thoughts are dark and dreary
And my heart is full of pain,
Then I like to rise up early
While the family's still asleep,
When the sky is pink and pearly
And the robins start to cheep.
I walk out to see the flowers
While the grass is wet with dew,
In the quiet morning hours
When the world looks fresh and new.

Then my heart can't help but lighten
When I see the beauty there,
As the colors slowly brighten
In the cool and misty air.
The crimson roses climbing
On the trellis spread perfume,
And the pink clematis twining
Helps to free my heart of gloom.

Then I lift my thoughts to heaven,
Give my fears to God above,
For the beauty He has given
Reassures me of His love.
And the terrors of the midnight,
Which had filled my heart with woe,
In the early morning sunlight
Lose their strength and slowly go.

An abundance of beautiful flowers welcomes visitors to this house in Rockport Cape, Massachusetts. Photograph by Mary Liz Austin/Donnelly Austin Photography.

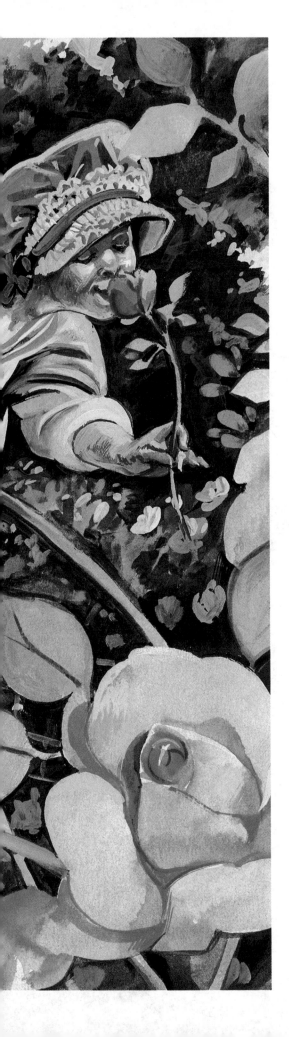

FOR THE CHILDREN

Busy Bee

Eileen Spinelli

Bee is busy in my garden
    buzzing round the mint and chive,
    sipping nectar from the roses,
    back and forth from bloom to hive.

Bee goes dancing deep in clover,
    visits my begonia bed,
    blossom shaking, honey making—
    Bee has lots of work ahead.

I am buzzing round my garden,
    chasing beetles, shaking dirt,
    snipping sprigs of dill and parsley,
    giving thirsty ferns a squirt.

Back and forth from beans to pepper,
    set the basket on the shelf,
    sweep the path and heap the clippings—
    I'm a busy bee myself!

Original artwork by Russ Flint.

Back Home

Anne Campbell

Back home the rows of tasseled corn,
Like stalwart knights of old,
Are marching in the silver morn,
Their pockets filled with gold.

Back home the clover-scented air
Is bathed in morning dew,
And winding through the woodlands there
Are joyous paths we knew.

Back home the lazy creek runs on
Between the maple trees,
And robins wake to send at dawn
A message to the breeze.

Back home, there once were roses wild
That for my sake leaned down
To whisper to a little child
With questing eyes of brown.

Back home the rambling weathered walls
Were bright with climbing flowers;
But silent are the empty halls,
And heavy are the hours.

For gone is each familiar trace.
In dreams alone I roam
To find the loveliness and grace
That touched each day, back home.

The attractive roofline of a barn with a cupola rises above a garden of lilies and gladioli in Rumney, New Hampshire. Photograph by William H. Johnson.

When Summer Corn Is Sweet

Inez Franck

The greening rows are rhymes of peace
Across the countryside;
They speak their joys in metaphors
Where rainbows hover wide.

The sun-glad skies look down with thanks
Upon the grain-filled ears,
As crickets chatter merrily
Like summer souvenirs.

Here is the feel of lyric days
And blessings so complete;
My heart belongs to country fields
When summer corn is sweet.

The sylvan slopes with corn-clad fields
Are hung, as if with golden shields,
Bright trophies of the sun!
    —William Wordsworth

Rows of corn and an octagonal barn make a
pleasing geometric design in the countryside.
Photograph by Mary Liz Austin/Donnelly
Austin Photography.

SLICE OF LIFE
Edna Jaques

MIDSUMMER PARADISE

Green verdure where old fences hide their feet;
    A one-horse wagon plodding up a hill;
A farmer hoeing in a field of corn
    Beside a creek whose song is never still;

A vine-clad porch; tall maples bending low;
    A wooden pump painted a homey red;
Scrub oak and hazel brush in bright array,
    Their tangled branches meeting overhead;

A wood thrush sending up a song of praise,
    Its little face up-tilted to the sky;
A quiet pasture with its sheltering elms
    And cool green hollows where the cattle lie;

A spring where crystal waters bubble up
    And overflow to form a tiny pool,
Where woodland elves might hide amid the ferns
    Near where the twenty froggies went to school—

Blessed is the land where peace and plenty dwell,
    Where little children wander hand in hand,
Heirs of a country rich beyond compare,
    Fortunate pilgrims of a happy land.

Summer's golden bounty is corn fresh from the field, as presented in the painting by Robert Duncan entitled CORN ON THE COB. *Image provided by Robert Duncan Studios. Copyright © Robert Duncan. All rights reserved.*

The Flavor of Sunshine

Ralph W. Seager

Corn is the model of America. It was the Indian's truth and the Pilgrim's riddle. It is the best multiplication table we know. A field of corn is more than corn; there are pigs and chickens in it—often literally! But always it means ham and eggs, bacon, and chicken legs. An ear of corn is a typewriter with golden keys that spells out taste in ecstasies. Upright, it is the Empire State building with every window lit, and you can hold it in your hand. It is fried pone and hot johnnycake, and with these in his mouth a man tells the truth when he says that he has tasted paradise.

My father was a good grower of sweet corn—sunshine by the conefull—all wrapped in green. He ran his hills north to south, the right way. The eastern side of day laid tenderness upon the ears, and the western side poured warmth upon them. When the valley put out its lights and went to bed, the moon and stars took over and the corn grew right on through the night. The moon would not let the corn forget the color of gold, and the stars put a twinkle upon every tassel. Warm nights are kind to corn.

I was in my tenth May when Dad planted his rows of sunshine on Decoration Day. I helped him drop these wrinkled multiplication tables, five to a hill. He covered them over and told me to jump back out of the way because corn grows awfully fast and he did not want me to be knocked over!

What an example of multiplication! These hard, knotty problems going into the mind of the earth, then springing out and up, up, figuring all the time and coming out with the correct answers right from the back of the book. So complete and shining—no fractions—everything working out evenly. I would not be surprised to learn that corn grows by the square root.

When the last hill was planted, Dad walked over and turned me toward our house. He said that the rest was up to me—that I should practice running that distance until the corn was ripe. And he was right again, for as soon as the ears are picked, their sunshine begins to leak out.

Speed is the answer if you want to know what the flavor of sunlight is. The shortest possible moment between garden and kitchen must be calculated, and a young son is the best annihilator of time and distance yet known. So I ran until the marrow in my leg bones turned into lightning. My toes became acquainted with speed.

As I kept running, the corn became curious and rose higher and higher, watching me all the way to the kitchen door. This is the only plan that lets man know the taste of the sun. "Store-boughten" corn cannot do it—not even the neighbor's corn will be right—it must come from one's own garden, and it is important to have a slim son to do the running.

We moved into the center of summer and things became important, became serious. The tassels began to flake apart, and Dad kept fingering the dark, rich silks. I felt wings gathering around my feet, and excitement was upon each of us. The day arrived—the best one since Genesis, Dad proclaimed with the sound of a prophet.

The womenfolk let the kitchen know what was going to happen. The stove got into the act; the boiling kettle quivered through its rehearsals; and the table waited, all set with plates, knives, butter, and salt. And sunshine stood straight up a hundred yards away.

Dad and I strode out of the kitchen and disappeared into the green rows. Grandma stayed by the door, hand to latch, ready to hurry me through when I came back. With wisdom in his fingers, Dad snapped off the golden batons and piled them into my arms. He whacked the seat of my pants and yelled, "Go!"

I was off on the final relay. I burst out of the long-leafed forest, one jump to the left over a hurdle of pumpkin vines, coming straightaway between the ruby rows of beets, flashing into the long sprint down the fern-trails the carrots made. Every wild thing ran with me. Deer were racing alongside. The quick trout was at my ankles. Hawks circled about my head. I was every creature with speed in his name.

As I kept running, the corn became curious and rose higher and higher, watching me all the way to the kitchen door.

Out from the last row of beans, I broke into a headlong dash that whipped across the backyard, up three steps in one leap, past Grandma, and through the kitchen door to spill the golden yield out onto the table.

The green jackets were zipped off, and the kitchen filled with dancing. Grandma danced. Mother danced. The kettle danced. The old stove did a jig, and the woodbox clogged. And not a precious moment was lost. Into the steaming mist, the bubbling waters, and all was safe. Sunshine had been caught in the act and sealed tight!

Dad's heavier steps thundered into the room, and we rushed to our places at the table. The kitchen became our universe, with sweet corn at its center. No one said a word. There is not much to say when you are in the middle of glory. A finger-burning glory, dripping with butter and smacking of salt, shone around us. Our teeth were deep in sunlight—the flavor of sunshine was on our tongues—the sun itself was in our mouths.

Photograph by Gay Bumgarner.

The Taste of Summer

Jean Stovall Earnest

The wild taste of the mountain
Is saved up in summer jars:
The tangy taste of huckleberry,
Preserved like blue-white stars;
Wild crab apples glowing
In jelly's golden gleam;
Jam made from blackberries
That grew along the stream;
The cool, crisp taste of purple
In the mountain streams' wild grapes;
Wild chokecherries gathered
With mountain winds' quick rakes;
Elderberry, wild strawberry,
And knotty possum pear,
Along with fruits from the orchard,
Wait by the cellar stair.

When the mountain is covered with snow
And the path's too slippery to climb—
Spread on a golden biscuit,
Summer's bright memories will shine.

Summer pastimes include an inviting backyard picnic. Photograph by Dianne Dietrich Leis/Dietrich Leis Stock Photography.

From America's Attic

D. Fran Morley

Jewels in a Jar

My mother once said having home-canned produce was like saving summer in a jar. I agreed with her on those cold winter days when we would open a jar of bright yellow peaches. Memories of warm summer days would come flooding back into me with every sweet bite. By then, I had forgotten the hard work that went into "putting up" the peaches and other garden produce that filled the jars lined up in neat rows on our pantry shelves.

My mother canned because her mother and her grandmother before her had done so. Today, I prepare home-canned jellies and relishes for nostalgia or as gifts for friends and family. When I have an abundance of green beans or corn from the garden, I will put some away in the freezer, but I do not consider it a necessity, as people did in the days before we had grocery stores on every corner and the convenience of fresh frozen foods.

Home canning is a relatively recent development, less than two hundred years old, but women have long had ways to preserve food in order to feed their families during the long winter months.

In her first book, *Little House in the Big Woods,* Laura Ingalls Wilder describes how her mother tended a smoldering fire in a hollow, upright log to smoke hams and venison that she later wrapped in paper and hung from the attic rafters. The family stored salted fish in barrels, made rich cheeses out of fresh milk, and preserved all the goodness of the summer garden, as Laura recalls. "Now the potatoes and carrots, the beets and turnips and cabbages were gathered and stored in the cellar, for freezing nights had come. Onions were made into long ropes, braided

---

Today's most familiar glass jar was introduced in 1883 by five brothers named Ball.

---

together by their tops, and then were hung in the attic beside wreaths of red peppers strung on threads. The pumpkins and the squashes were piled in orange and yellow and green heaps in the attic's corners. The little house was fairly bursting with good food stored away for the long winter. The pantry and the shed and the cellar were full, and so was the attic." Living in the woods of Wisconsin in the 1870s, Caroline Ingalls would have preserved foods by pickling, drying, smoking, and salting—all methods that women have used for centuries to keep food safe to eat.

The process of canning foods dates back to the late 1700s to Napoleon, who paid a sizable reward to the inventor that devised this improved method to preserve meat and vegetables. It is likely that Caroline Ingalls would have known about this new process. She may have

Photograph by Fred Habegger/Grant Heilman.

dill pickles. When these so-called Mason Jars were processed in boiling water, a thin rubber ring on the inside of the lid created a tight seal.

Other inventors added to the inventory of jars. In 1882, a Vermont inventor created a fruit jar with a glass lid and an attached metal clamp that held the lid in place. Called Lightning Jars because they were so quick and easy to open and close, these jars were adopted by home canners who used them with great regularity through the 1960s. They still have a nostalgic value today, although it is more common to see Lightning Jars filled with cotton balls on a bathroom counter than green beans in a pantry.

Today's most familiar glass jar was introduced in 1883 by five brothers named Ball, who had a glass factory in Muncie, Indiana. The Ball brothers made no major changes to jar style; but, with mass production and distribution around the country and eventually around the world, they were able to quickly make their jars a household favorite.

A few years later after the Ball jars were in production, Alexander Kerr introduced a new innovation to home canning with his creation of the two-part lids that are still used today. Kerr's disposable flat metal discs, held in place by reusable metal rings, made canning less expensive and more convenient than ever before.

Home canning is now much easier than in years past. Like my mother and grandmothers before me, I still have to stand over a boiling pot of water and pots of steaming vegetables, but I have the convenience of doing so in an air-conditioned kitchen—a luxury they may not have imagined. And even though canning is only a hobby to me, it is still satisfying to know that the fruits and vegetables of my garden labor have been safely stored away. The joy of opening a jar of home-canned peaches still brings a bit of summer sunshine into a snowy winter's day.

even purchased canned goods from time to time, but home canning with glass jars would have been difficult on the frontier.

Sealing the jar safely has always been a major concern. Originally, home-canning jars had straight, smooth sides similar to a drinking glass; a material like pitch or sealing wax was used to hold flat, tin lids in place. The process was messy and did not always create a reliable seal. In 1858, a tinsmith named James Mason invented and patented a glass jar with a thread molded into its top and a threaded lid that screwed onto the jar—very much like the common jar that we see today filled with everything from mayonnaise to

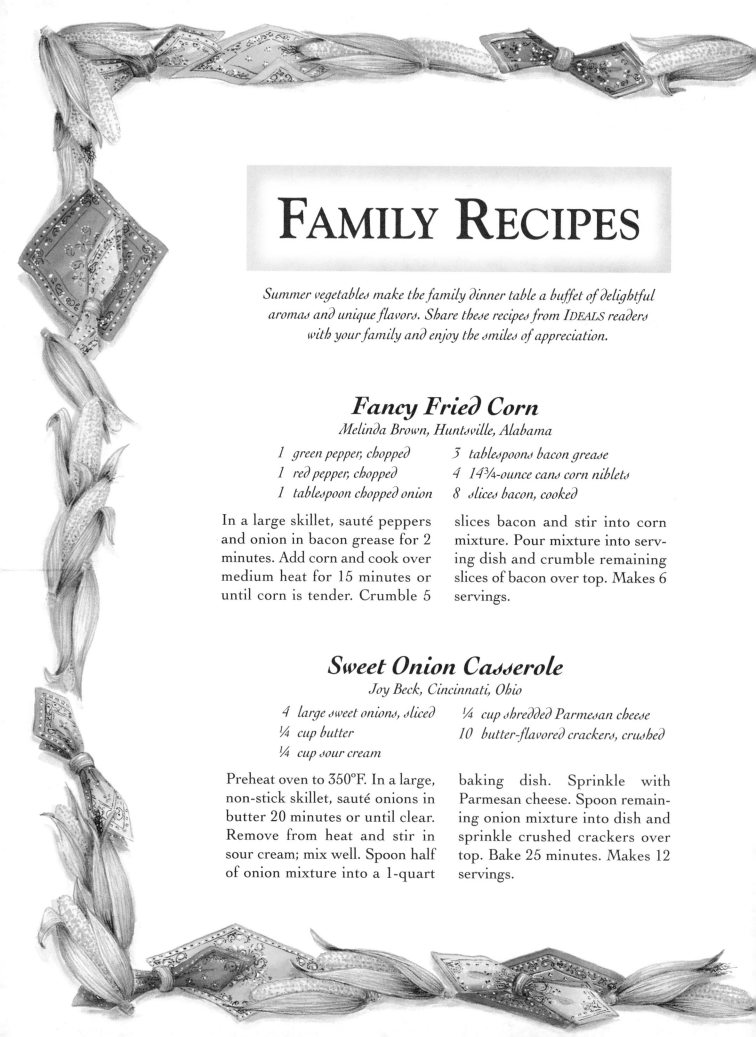

FAMILY RECIPES

Summer vegetables make the family dinner table a buffet of delightful aromas and unique flavors. Share these recipes from IDEALS readers with your family and enjoy the smiles of appreciation.

Fancy Fried Corn

Melinda Brown, Huntsville, Alabama

1 green pepper, chopped
1 red pepper, chopped
1 tablespoon chopped onion
3 tablespoons bacon grease
4 14¾-ounce cans corn niblets
8 slices bacon, cooked

In a large skillet, sauté peppers and onion in bacon grease for 2 minutes. Add corn and cook over medium heat for 15 minutes or until corn is tender. Crumble 5 slices bacon and stir into corn mixture. Pour mixture into serving dish and crumble remaining slices of bacon over top. Makes 6 servings.

Sweet Onion Casserole

Joy Beck, Cincinnati, Ohio

4 large sweet onions, sliced
¼ cup butter
¼ cup sour cream
¼ cup shredded Parmesan cheese
10 butter-flavored crackers, crushed

Preheat oven to 350°F. In a large, non-stick skillet, sauté onions in butter 20 minutes or until clear. Remove from heat and stir in sour cream; mix well. Spoon half of onion mixture into a 1-quart baking dish. Sprinkle with Parmesan cheese. Spoon remaining onion mixture into dish and sprinkle crushed crackers over top. Bake 25 minutes. Makes 12 servings.

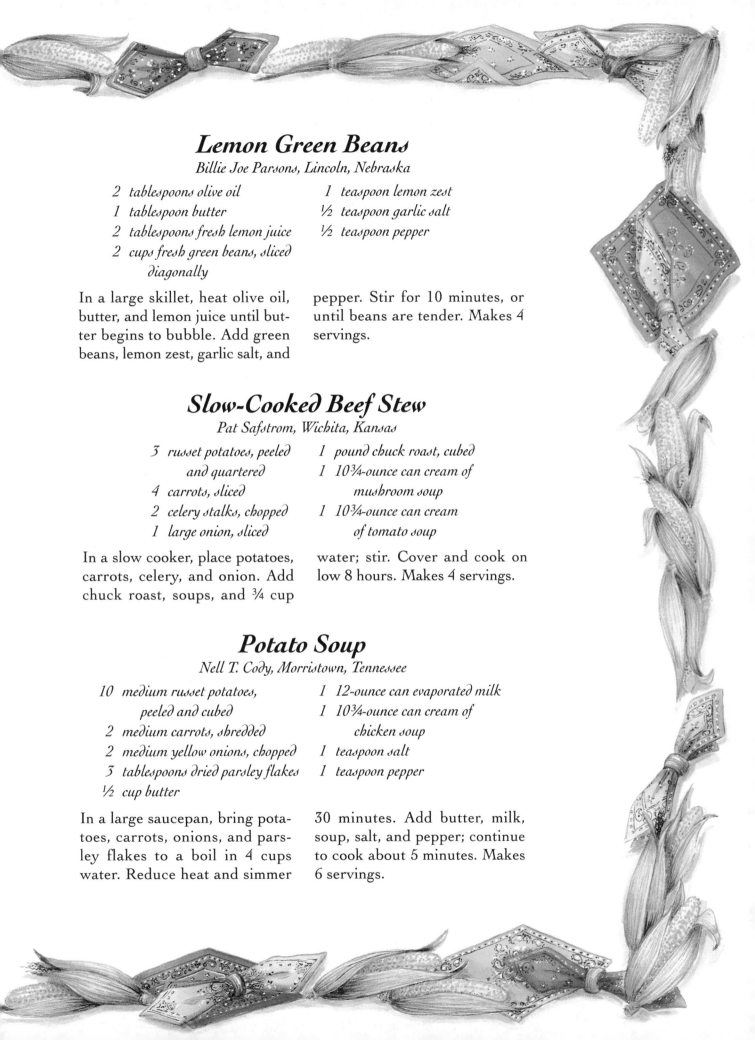

Lemon Green Beans

Billie Joe Parsons, Lincoln, Nebraska

2 tablespoons olive oil
1 tablespoon butter
2 tablespoons fresh lemon juice
2 cups fresh green beans, sliced diagonally
1 teaspoon lemon zest
½ teaspoon garlic salt
½ teaspoon pepper

In a large skillet, heat olive oil, butter, and lemon juice until butter begins to bubble. Add green beans, lemon zest, garlic salt, and pepper. Stir for 10 minutes, or until beans are tender. Makes 4 servings.

Slow-Cooked Beef Stew

Pat Safstrom, Wichita, Kansas

3 russet potatoes, peeled and quartered
4 carrots, sliced
2 celery stalks, chopped
1 large onion, sliced
1 pound chuck roast, cubed
1 10¾-ounce can cream of mushroom soup
1 10¾-ounce can cream of tomato soup

In a slow cooker, place potatoes, carrots, celery, and onion. Add chuck roast, soups, and ¾ cup water; stir. Cover and cook on low 8 hours. Makes 4 servings.

Potato Soup

Nell T. Cody, Morristown, Tennessee

10 medium russet potatoes, peeled and cubed
2 medium carrots, shredded
2 medium yellow onions, chopped
3 tablespoons dried parsley flakes
½ cup butter
1 12-ounce can evaporated milk
1 10¾-ounce can cream of chicken soup
1 teaspoon salt
1 teaspoon pepper

In a large saucepan, bring potatoes, carrots, onions, and parsley flakes to a boil in 4 cups water. Reduce heat and simmer 30 minutes. Add butter, milk, soup, salt, and pepper; continue to cook about 5 minutes. Makes 6 servings.

DEVOTIONS FROM THE HEART

Pamela Kennedy

Remember this: Whoever sows sparingly will also reap sparingly, and whoever sows generously will also reap generously. —*2 Corinthians 9:6* (NIV)

So . . . How Do You Sow?

I have one of those screensavers on my computer that cycles through a variety of scenic vistas every few seconds. One day, when inspiration and motivation were particularly sparse, I sat staring at the screen, mesmerized by the beautiful scenery. Waving palms melted into tumbling surf, waterfalls splashed into pools that morphed into majestic mountains, and rippling streams flowed into fields of wheat, undulating in the summer wind.

It was the fields of wheat that brought to mind the verse above from Paul's second letter to the believers at Corinth. The wheat fields on my computer screen looked like they extended for miles. I began to wonder about the little seeds, millions of them, that must have been sown in the fertile soil of some Midwestern plain and about the farmers who planted them. Was that what Paul had envisioned as he penned his words? I suspect not, because the context of this verse has to do with giving and good works, not with agriculture. But it got me thinking about other kinds of sowing and harvests, and I'm pretty sure that's what Paul intended.

I began to look around at some of the planters in my community and at the harvests they are yielding. The school where I teach was planted over 135 years ago by a Hawaiian queen with a vision for educating young women. Since the initial sowing of Queen Emma's dream, generations of daughters have earned degrees from St. Andrew's Priory and gone on to serve as leaders in every field imaginable.

Another aspect of my life influenced by a

Dear Lord of the harvest, please help me to be a diligent and joyful planter so that the seeds I sow will produce abundant blessings in the lives I touch every day. Amen.

planter is the area where I live; it was a tropical jungle only forty-five years ago. Then a wealthy developer named Henry Kaiser—who combined his two passions to create a new word, *imagineering*—designed and built a planned community with ponds, canals, and homes for thousands of families. His generously planted seeds grew into Hawaii Kai, a thriving suburb twelve miles east of Honolulu.

The more I looked, the more I found. There are generous sowers all around me. A best friend is the children's director at our church. Every

Photograph by Terry Donnelly/Donnelly Austin Photography.

week she leads a team of teachers who plant seeds of faith and encouragement in the lives of their young students. A colleague tutors young women who are incarcerated, planting seeds of hope for a more productive future. A retired executive works tirelessly to acquire resources to build housing and clinics for the homeless. A young couple spends their vacation planting vegetable gardens in the poorest shantytowns of South Africa. Harvests are springing up everywhere.

And then I discovered something about that verse of Paul's I had never seen before: We are all sowers. He doesn't say some are sowers and some are not. He says some sow sparingly and some sow generously. We're all planting every day!

The choice then becomes one of deciding the kind of harvest we want to produce. If I want to leave a legacy that perpetuates blessing, I need to be generously planting seeds of faith and joy, of encouragement and hope every day. Seeds of negativity, criticism, anger, or worry only lead to scrawny weeds of discouragement.

Thinking of myself as a sower gives me a new perspective on my everyday encounters. There is fertile soil all around, people ready to receive a word or smile, planted with kindness and watered with loving patience. We each have the exciting and challenging opportunity to become a partner with God, who prepares the soil and superintends the harvest. Then together we can enjoy the fruitfulness of His grace. It doesn't matter if we are royalty, millionaires, teachers, executives, or homemakers. I now realize that whatever we are, we are also sowers. Each day, the fields await us, prepared and ready. So . . . how do you sow?

Harvest

Esther Loewen Vogt

Like endless seas, the golden grain is teeming
As June winds, softly rippling, blow;
The cobalt sky, bluer still is seeming
While fleeced clouds gently come and go.
The harvesters are cutting swathes of treasure,
With patience by the farmer sown;
And now the time of reaping in good measure
Has come again, to each his own.

Whatever we sow, we shall some day be reaping—
Be it our deeds, our thoughts, or grain.
And he that goes forth one day with weeping
Shall doubtless come home with joy again.

Americana

Dean Robbins

There stands in Pennsylvania, on a hill,
A weathered tractor—silent, strong, and still—
Beneath a flag that waves upon the breeze;
And all America I see in these.

The tractor might have roamed surrounding fields
Depended on once for plentiful yields
Of corn or wheat, but which kiss the wind today
As acres of some farmer's winter hay.

The flag, though worn, flies ever tall and proud,
Set off against the occasional cloud
Billowing white in skies of powder blue,
While stars and stripes swear honor, tried and true.

I've seen things I've forgotten in a day
And those which in my mind shall stay,
Returning in a random thought, as will
That sight in Pennsylvania on a hill.

Waves of amber grain flow with the summer breezes at Bishop Farm in Ebey's Landing National Historic Reserve on Whidby Island, Washington. Photograph by Mary Liz Austin/Donnelly Austin Photography.

ONE FLAG, ONE LAND, ONE HEART, ONE HAND,
ONE NATION EVERMORE!

—OLIVER WENDELL HOLMES

MY FLAG

Lucille Crumley

I see my flag, high-flying there,
Blowing free in the summer air.
A bit of cloth in red, white, and blue—
But, oh, the things my flag can do.
It can rally men when a cause is lost
To heroic deeds whatever the cost.
It can speak with a shout, whisper a sigh,
Quiet a crowd, bring tears to the eye.
Men do not cower, but stand proud instead,
When this fold of cloth, this bit of thread,
Flutters free as it passes by—
My beautiful, beautiful flag, flying high.

OUR FLAG

Bessie H. Hartling

It speaks in steadfast color:
The red, the white, the blue;
It tells us what to honor:
The brave, the pure, the true.

It graces its staff with beauty,
Enlivens the languid air;
It drapes our country's heroes
And wafts a graveside prayer.

It guards our home of worship
And crowns our courts and schools,
Proclaiming the law of liberty,
The heart of freedom's rules.

We stand at grave attention
To salute our nation's pride,
Our flag of cherished history
For which dear sons have died.

*A flag flies at the entrance to an inn on Nantucket
Island. Photograph by William H. Johnson.*

VALLEY FORGE

Grace Noll Crowell

We know so little, we forget so much
Of our country's history of long ago.
Let us go with Washington to Valley Forge
And face the bitter wind, the blinding snow,
The ragged clothing, the frostbitten feet,
The disheartened men, too ill at times to stand.
Yet every hardship that they bore was shared
By the sympathetic leader in command.
He built into the fabric of a dream
The fact that this, our country, could be great.
He shared that dream with others, some who found
Its bright fulfillment coming all too late.
He suffered for that dream; he fought a fight
That tore the heart with anguish and distress.
He strove for a nation's glorious destiny
With a steadfast faith of ultimate success—
A faith that blossomed like a hardy flower
Out of the bitter soil of that dark hour.

America has furnished to the world the character of Washington! And if our American institutions had done nothing else, that alone would have entitled them to the respect of mankind.

—Daniel Webster

George Washington's headquarters stand at Valley Forge, Pennsylvania.
Photograph by J. McGrail/H. Armstrong Roberts.

*The secret of happiness is freedom,
and the secret of freedom, courage.*
—THUCYDIDES

God Grant Us Wisdom

Genie Makinster

Oh, for the wisdom to build a world
Where man may find delight,
Not in the strength of martial power,
But in the quest for truth and right.
We would not ask that the way be cleared
And smoothed for our eager feet;
But, rather, freedom from groundless fear,
So our problems we may meet.
Yes, ours is a prayer for freedom, for strength,
And for opportunity
In a world not only of toil and tears,
But of love and liberty.

*To every man his chance;
To every man, regardless of his birth, his shining, golden opportunity;
To every man the right to live, to work, to be himself, and to become
whatever his manhood and his vision can combine to make him—
This, seeker, is the promise of America.*
—THOMAS WOLFE

*Fireweed envelops the banks of Canada's Tatshenshini River, in British Columbia.
Photograph by Carr Clifton.*

READERS' REFLECTIONS

Come Sing with Me
Marilyn Hinson
Lilburn, Georgia

Come sing with me of being free,
Of fluffy clouds above the sea,
Billowing, swirling, as if at play,
Reflecting soft colors at the close of day.

Come sing with me of soft, white sand,
Of friends together, walking hand in hand,
Of a shoreline stretching far and wide,
Of the moon and stars at eveningtide.

Shells scatter on the beach, washed in by tides—
Not so different from our own lives;
Each shell separate, no two the same,
Though mingled together, each has its own name.

Come sing with me of each man's worth,
A right we have from time of birth;
We all are different, no two the same;
Yet God knows each of us by our name.

America's Castles
Lorraine E. Mitchell
Hatboro, Pennsylvania

We who live in America
Cherish no crumbling towers;
We have no castles turreted,
And palaces are not ours.

Instead we follow winding roads
And marvel at mountains' height;
We love the ever-rolling sea
Beneath faithful beacon light.

Our tall, old towers sturdy stand
Through long centuries and more:
Our castles are the lighthouses
That guard our miles-long shores.

Our Flag Forever

Evelyn Steen Taylor
Monroe, Louisiana

Stand behind the flag,
Wherever it might be,
For it flies as a symbol
Representing you and me.

Down through all the ages
Of peace or bitter strife,
The tricolored badge of America
Has reigned over death and life.

Let it always instill courage,
Upholding freedom's dream;
And when the world dismays,
Let it shine a guiding beam.

May America be blessed,
As from the days gone by;
May her people stand with pride
And the flag forever fly.

Fourth of July

Peggy L. Brady
New Britain, Pennsylvania

We gather to join in sweet freedom's song,
Free still to express our view;
It's another Fourth of July,
Our country's birthday, yet so new.

The marching band is warming up;
There's very little shade;
The street is lined with people
Awaiting the big parade.

This country that we call home
Is the best beyond compare;
On this, its birthday,
We join hands and hearts and share.

In past battles that love has fought,
We remember the many brave we've lost.
Though sad, we vow to keep home safe,
No matter what the cost.

See there, in our American sky,
Majesty that taught us to pray.
Old Glory still proudly waves on high—
Happy Birthday, USA!

Oh, the summer night
Has a smile of light,
And she sits on a sapphire throne.
—Barry Cornwall

Summer Stars
Carl Sandburg

Bend low again, night of summer stars.
So near you are, sky of summer stars,
So near, a long arm man can pick off stars,
Pick off what he wants in the sky bowl,
So near you are, summer stars,
So near, strumming, strumming,
So lazy and humstrumming.

Crickets at Dawn
Leonora Speyer

All night the crickets chirp,
Like little stars of twinkling sound
In the dark silence.

They sparkle through the summer stillness
With a crisp rhythm:
They lift the shadows on their tiny voices.

But at the shining note of birds that wake,
Flashing from tree to tree till all the wood is lit—
O golden coloratura of dawn!
The cricket-stars fade slowly,
One by one.

The lighthouse at Ninini Beach overlooks the turquoise water at Nawiliwili Bay on Kauai, Hawaii. Photograph by Terry Donnelly/Donnelly Austin Photography.

BACKYARD CALENDAR

Joan Donaldson

A shower of rose petals falls on John and me as we duck beneath the blossom-laden branches that cover the garden gate. After a stretch of humid days, the crisp evening air has drawn us out to stroll the garden paths and note the progress of plants.

"Couldn't you prune these lower branches?" John teases. He has come to accept my penchant for climbing roses, but wishes that I would measure their height by his taller stature.

"Listen." I divert the question. A wood thrush sings from the sassafras trees that embrace the northern fence of the garden, celebrating the respite from the heat with his honey-sweet voice.

John wanders off to inspect his melons, while I lift a drooping tomato branch and weave it upward through a homemade trellis of baling twine. Several years ago, I discovered this method of stringing a warp between metal stakes and threading the tomatoes through the strings. A green tapestry stretches down the row, dotted with yellow flowers reminiscent of last night's Fourth of July fireworks that exploded into brilliant blossoms. I arrange a plum-size tomato over a string and calculate how many more days I must wait until red flashes between the leaves.

The first fruits of the garden are the sweetest. Just as my family lounged on the beach anticipating the initial boom that heralded the first dazzle of fireworks, we eagerly wait for the arrival of each crop.

"I found the first watermelon," John calls, spreading apart the tangle of speckled leaves. A pistachio-green egg hides near the base of the plant. "And this plant has a cantaloupe the size of a softball. Did you look at the broccoli? It should be ready in a few days."

Beads of water glisten in the crevices of the crumpled surface of the broccoli heads. By week's end, I will have cut most of these heads, and green packages will reside in my freezer. A few immature stragglers will escape my freezing frenzy and become food for the butterflies. I will watch the viceroy and the swallowtail, a swirl of orange

---

Beets and beans, cucumbers and summer squash will soon fill my baskets as the plants expand, the leaves toppling over the paths.

---

and yellow, hover above the plants before drifting over the pink florets of valerian next to the wooden fence. Come winter, the memory of their wings will tickle my senses each time I open a frosty bag of broccoli and smell summer.

"I just ate a bean," John quips. "Only two inches long, but tasty. When will you can beets? Can't wait for some borscht." Beets and beans, cucumbers and summer squash will soon fill my baskets as the plants expand, the leaves toppling over the paths. Today we relish the early ruby

A butterfly is delighted with the pastel blooms of Robin's plantain in this garden. Photograph by William H. Johnson.

globes and the smooth-skinned squash, stir-fried with basil. But as July slides by and the heat waves ripple, I vow that next year I will plant shorter rows of beans. I will sprinkle cosmos and zinnia seeds next to the beets and send more bouquets home with visiting friends instead of Savoy cabbage. Yet, most likely at Christmas, when I place jars of pickled beets in my friends' hands, I will remember the joy of sharing from this year's abundant harvest.

A swallowtail pauses on a lavender blossom, tipping an anise hyssop plant that some bird planted near our sundial. The yellow butterfly opens and closes its wings while it sips, as if to thank me for leaving this source of nectar instead of clearing this volunteer while weeding the carrots.

A faint scent of licorice rises from the gray-green leaves. The last golden rays of the sunset illuminate John's face as he emerges from inspect-

ing the sweet corn. Tassels flecked with pollen rise from the shoulder-high stalks, which confirm that the pace of summer has quickened.

"Two, three more weeks and that early variety will be ripe. Can't wait for the first bite of sweet corn." John takes my hand, and we walk toward the gate.

"And neither can I." I latch the gate behind us. We will savor each fresh tomato and pungent melon, grateful for the sun, the rain, and the earth that bring these first fruits into our lives, and the pleasure we share watching our garden grow.

Joan Donaldson is the author of books for children and young adults, as well as essays that have appeared in national publications. She and her husband raised their sons on Pleasant Hill Farm in Michigan, where they continue to practice rural skills.

READERS' FORUM

Snapshots from our IDEALS readers

Left: "I miss you," says two-year-old Alexis Kennedy Hopkins in a make-believe conversation with her mother before going to bed one night at church camp. Her grandmother, Virginia Switzer of Louisville, Kentucky, shares this photograph with IDEALS readers. Alexis is the younger sister of Alexander and daughter of Charlton and Larinda Hopkins.

Below left: "Daisies, daisies, everywhere, tickle my nose and cuddle my toes." Anna McCourry of Burnsville, North Carolina, shares this snapshot of her grandson, two-year-old David Ethan.

Below right: "Ready to jump?" Twins Chance and Lance Sheets pause for a snapshot, just before toppling into trouble. Grandmother Faye H. Sheets of Marlinton, West Virginia, shares this wonderful moment.

Above: Two-year-old Erin Holland fits perfectly into her turtle sandbox. She is the younger sister of Courtney and daughter of Tim and Missy Holland of Fletcher, North Carolina. Her proud grandparents are Charles and Mary Parker.

Right: "I'm ready to fly!" Two-year-old Karen Durbin clutches her surprise balloon bouquet as tightly as she can, during a visit to her grandmother's house. Her mother is Cherie Durbin of Hickory, North Carolina.

Below: Kirby cousins Bennett, Grace, Emily, and Mary Ellen picnic on the same rock by the same creek their fathers once enjoyed. Great-Grandmother Blanche Dugan of Fayetteville, North Carolina, sent this snapshot to IDEALS.

Dear Reader,

My father was tall and slender, and Mother often accused him of being slightly deaf because his normal conversational tone was rather loud. He never sat still except to read. I remember many days he came home for lunch and read for thirty minutes.

As the oldest of three sons, my father worked long hours as a painter in order to put himself through college and then law school. He served in the military in the Pacific during World War II and later Germany.

When my father decided to run for public office, our house was filled with people dropping in for informal meetings, and the phone seemed to ring continuously. He would practice his speeches in front of Mother and me; then he would laugh and say that if we did not like it, the speech was sure to be a success. He worked hard to attract industry to our small town and then welcomed the new residents into our home. I can recall few weekends that my parents were not having people for dinner or going to a friend's house.

My father was an honest man. He never took advantage of his position in business or politics to accumulate wealth. His was the generation that actually conducted business with a handshake.

My father showed his love through actions rather than words. On my fourth birthday, he brought home a small black puppy, saying one of his customers just couldn't take care of her, but he knew I would. We hosted an exchange student from France for a year. Since Marie José's own father had died when she was young, Dad welcomed her into his heart and for the rest of his life referred to her as his "French daughter." He cried at both our weddings.

When my father hugged me or said he was proud of me, I knew the world was a good place. I miss him every day.

Marjorie L. Lloyd

Publisher, Patricia A. Pingry
Editor, Marjorie Lloyd
Designer, Royce DeGrie
Copy Editors, Melinda Rathjen, Nancy Skarmeas
Permissions Editor, Patsy Jay
Contributing Writers, Lansing Christman, Joan Donaldson, Pamela Kennedy, D. Fran Morley

ACKNOWLEDGMENTS

BURKET, GAIL BROOK. "Thank You, Father." Used by permission of Anne E. Burket. BUTLER, EDITH SHAW. "A Day Up River." Used by permission of Nancy B. Truesdell. CHRISTMAN, LANSING. "Old Barns" from *Harp Strings In the Wind*. Copyright © 1998. Used by permission of the author. CROWELL, GRACE NOLL. "Valley Forge" from *The Gold Star Family Album*, 1966, published by Fleming Revell. Used by permission of Claire Cumberworth. CRUMLEY, LUCILLE MCBROOM. "Honeysuckle" and "My Flag." Used by permission of Jane Cragin. FARR, HILDA BUTLER. "My Father." Used by permission of Heather Fuchslin, Attorney-in-Fact for Elsie Farr Day. FIELD, RUTH. "Golden Day." Used by permission of Natalie Field Bevis. FRANK, INEZ. "When Summer Corn Is Sweet." Used by permission of Caroline F. Stevens. JAQUES, EDNA. "Mid-Summer Paradise." Used by permission of Louise Bonnell. LARSON, LAVERNE. "The Country Path." Used by permission of Maureen E. Walsh. NANCE, BERTA HART. "Treasures" from *The Dallas Morning News*, 1926. Used here with no objection. SHARPE, ERNEST JACK. "Simple Things" from *136 Narratives of Nature*. Used by permission of Nancy L. Harper for the White Cloud Community Library. We sincerely thank those authors, or their heirs, some of whom we were unable to locate, who submitted original poems or articles to *Ideals* for publication. Every possible effort has been made to acknowledge ownership of material used.

Inside back cover: Delicate flowers border a small waterfall in this painting entitled ALPINE FLOWERS BY A STREAM by Otto Didrik Ottesen (1816–1982). Image from Fine Art Photographic Library, Ltd., London/ Eaton Gallery, London.